JEFFREY FILBERT

THE HAT I WEAR ON THE INSIDE OF MY HEAD

Poetry and Prints

Boston • 2022

Jeffrey Filbert

The Hat I Wear on the Inside of My Head
Poetry and Prints

Copyright © 2022 by Jeffrey Filbert

All rights reserved. No part of this book may be reproduced or utilized in any form or by any means, electronic or mechanical, including photocopying, recording, or by any information storage and retrieval system, without the written permission of the copyright holder(s).

ISBN 978-1-950319886
Library of Congress Control Number: 2022941653

Book Design and Layout by Julia Grushko © 2022

Painting by Jeffrey Filbert
Cover: "New Face" / 70"×70", Silkscreens on canvas
Back cover: "Self-Portrait" / 10"×12", Oil on canvas

Published by M·Graphics | Boston, MA
  www.mgraphics-books.com
  mgraphics.books@gmail.com

Printed in the United States of America

Contents

Landscape Music 8
Camden 1985 11
Whitman's Neighbor 12
Proportions 15
Work 17
Demo 18
Early Days 19
Ask 19
Studio Morning 22
Concert 24
Concert II 26
Aged 13 and 20 28
The Roads of the Face 31
Love or Something Like It 32
Of the Phenomenon of Age 34
Jays 35
The Moon at Dusk 36
August 20th 37
10PM 38
Way In 42
Way Out 43
Farewell Dusk 46
Hidden Words 50
Birthmark 52
A Possible Good-Bye 53
Way In: Monday Morning, Week of Storms 54
Backyard Clean Up 56
Acceptance 59
"I can't keep up with the reckoning…" 60

"Climbing up and down the rocky slopes..." 61
Way In: Saturday. 62
sOrrOw. 64
Posthumously Written Poem 65
Dear Despair, ... 66
Fra Angelico 67
Winter Morning 68
The Steps 70
Cello Bits. 74
"Listening to the opera always transforms the studio..." 75
The First Movement 76
Flea Market 79
Nowhere To Go. 80
Beginning, Middle, End 83
Maybe 85
Hopscotch 88
So Be It 91
12.22.12. 93
Mar. 12 95
Summer Nights 96
Student Days Still Life Hours 98
Painter 99
Tintoretto 100
Way In 108
An Intricate Pattern 110
Rain 111
What if... 112
Pool 114
As a Kid 115
The Canoe of Our Bones 116
Auto-Portrait 118
An Old Photograph 119
Snow Day 120
Wet Feet 122

The Concrete Body Made of Light	126
High Point Trail, February Residency, Peter's Valley	129
Like a Full Moon	130
Fever Day 3	132
The Request	134
The News	135
Scaffolding	136
A History of Landscape	137
Museum	138
Lunch Time Poem	139
Under	140
Mandala	142
Opening the Window	144
Perspective	145
Starting Out and Continuing	146
Labyrinth	149
Hat	150
A Day	152
Amazement	154
The Clock	155
To Salem	156
A.G.	157
Resistance	159
Youth	161
July 5	162
America the Beautiful?	164
T V	165
Gloucester City Memorial	168
Black Horse Pike and Kings Highway	170
From Silence	171
Sequence	172
The Sea Is Writing Its Autobiography	174
Morning	177
Hi Dog	178

Landscape Music

A half-mile one-way and the continuous thread of Rt. 295's
Whisper or brawling rush hour.
Another direction the grinding steel rumble
And train horn blast at 6 am through the intersection
Near the Brass Rail. Overhead planes in a holding pattern
Search like flashlights through the sky
Until the thunder of descent into Philadelphia Airport.
The occasional car off to work.
A dog's bark.
The ignition of the engine turning over in Trish's driveway.
A squirrel scampering over the roof
Then smaller and smaller and even smaller sounds in the room.
Can I ever sleep again?
My head a storage shed of imagined paintings
That want to jump out all at once as if the shed was on fire.
The world is hot.
If I wasn't here
I'd be on the first bus
To be here.

HURRAH! AGAIN! IF I WASN'T HERE I'D BE ON THE FIRST BUS TO BE HERE

kick

wheel

spin

Clay

Zoom

smooth

harmoniously

wet

cylinder

rising

Camden 1985

Someone's sadness
Floated from the window sill
Like a paper plane
Against the fabulous shades of the sky.

That sudden world of isolation
Rushed against me like water up to my knees,
The beat up beauty of a deserted street
The burnt loaves of discarded bread
That are the battered faces of summer heat.

Whitman's Neighbor

I will always come back to my studio,
Its fields of planks of wood
And stone outcroppings of cinder block
With trails that snake down and around
Raw walls of canvas.

I will always come back to the sky
Its immense mutability
Of blue sea-sky blazing
Above blue sea.

I will come back to trees near an edge
With roots exposed, eroded, shining out of earth
Where we can go and see
Parts of our selves wash away.

I will come back to faces,
Eyes, nose, mouth,
The whole head like a jewel box
Holding consciousness.

I will come back to arms, legs,
Pointing north, south, east and west
In dance or love
As roads leading to some
Unorthodox horizon.

I will always come back
To the sweeping
Dresses of this world
Whether stone or flesh.

I will come back
Like a flower carrying
A mountain in its roots.

Proportions

The studio is shoebox proportion
Where I walk around like one shoe
Looking for the other.

    Buried in my palm
    Is a mound of dirt
    Fertilized with seeds
    Blown by the wind.

Everything seems possible, but,
Not right away, of course.
Wading up to your knees
In the bay,
You feel more, a part,
And not, apart.

Work

If you've worked all your life
Or for many years at something
You wanted or longed for
Weathering all opposition
And circumstances, in a very
Nice, even tender way, you
Begin to go crazy in how
Wonderful everything is.

Demo

Out by 5:30 a.m.
Going north along the Delaware River.
Then east on Rt. 90
That pulls in the center of Jersey
Like a tight belt in a cartoon.

Driving into the sunrise
Turning the radio on
Just as Appalachian Spring begins.

A one-day workshop
Held at Brick Township High School
Throwing on the potter's wheel.

What can I do in one day?
State money most would rather spend on facts.
Softballs of clay get
Thrown into cylinders
On home plate.
As the clay rises back's straighten
To watch as if they
Were pulled up like clay, too.
All I seem to be saying is
Joy is possible.

Early Days

After painting the bread
I ate it
Sometimes hungry
Eating the bread
As I painted it
Adjusting the painting
Accordingly,
Eventually ending up
With a facade
Like those buildings
In old cowboy movies

Ask

Three things that get heavy fast
Steel, dirt, water.
Ask my back.

Clay spinning my hands
like gloves over ancient hands
throwing emptiness

Studio Morning

Eastern morning light streams through
17 windows and 4 doors. The illusory world
Gently rises. Rusty wrought iron balconies
Face east and south. From either
I look out on to green fields where empty
Vandalized houses once stood like gravestones.
With doors ajar there's always a breeze
From the river easing summer heat
Where I work in its stream
Letting sanded plaster
Blow away from me.
The upstairs of the studio
Gestures equanimity.
In the new garden out back
Tomatoes and pumpkins grow tangled together.
I drink coffee at a worn
Slightly concave table
That was a marble step
History carved with shoes,
In the background the continuous
Rhythm of the building,

Breathing in and out its own story
Of spirituals and Chianti
As once church and Italian restaurant,
And now I have been here many years
And plan to be many more
Dreaming with hard work.

Concert

We are all in the audience
In our love affair
With Beethoven's 9th symphony.
Some are married to the violins,
Some to the pretty flute.
Some are pulled above themselves
As if on wires like a cloud
Or angel in a child's play.

If these sounds could be transcribed in stone
They would have the contoured astonishment
Of Michelangelo's last clawed Pietas.

In our seats we are the invisible mountain
Of the haiku poem—

"First there is a mountain
Then there is no mountain
Then there is"

Then, 'there is'
Comes whirling around again,
Like the beginning of a waterfall
Trickling down my neck
Then with momentum slipping
Over the rocks of my shoulder
As I step, step by step

Down the steppes to the lobbies
Acres and acres of pine.
And we all know he was deaf
When he wrote it.
Trading hearing sound
For hearing light.

Concert II

Bach is weaving an infallible
Flying carpet just above us,
2000 threads per square inch,
Strong enough to hold everybody
Dancing across it
As we ascend.

It is made of quarter notes and half note"s
Hooked and looped through
The spirals of treble clefs,
Then pulled taut, as if a loom
Was hidden up his sleeve.
Unlike a magicians
"There is nothing up my sleeve."

The concert over,
Our feet are back in this world
Just in time to stand for an ovation.
The conductor waves sections
Of the orchestra to stand and so,
Conducts too, the applause of the audience.

Eventually the musicians wander off
Through huge black rectangles off stage
Carrying the out-of-their-body voices.

Bach's hat has grown over time
That now it could be a cathedral dome
Painted with stars.

Aged 13 and 20

How could you not cry
For the suicided ones
Who could not figure it all
Would be past one day
And there always was the
Potential for happiness
Though one can't promise anything.

You have been been through enough
Time just to BE HAPPY

The Roads of the Face

The roads of the face
Can be difficult to read
So many need ask
How to get to the playground
Or the house of who you are.
Roads through the brush
Scar the verdant world.
Roads through cities
Are clotted veins.
I try to tear the roads
From my face saying
Here I am
But others are quickly laid
And sometimes I don't even know
My way home.

Love or Something Like It

Is in the flower
Giving it its color

**Love is not afraid of love.
Go guy kiss guy,
Go kiss girl to girl.
I do not know who
Loves who but I know
Do not interfere with love.**

Everywhere —

Between wind and tree.
Sky and mind, even
Joy and grief are entwined
On millions of unmade beds,
And the potentiality
Of men and women
Loving each other.

Of the Phenomenon of Age

The outer body leads to dark
The inner body leads to light,
If all goes well.

If, in your own way,
You have lived courageously,
Have found a path
That, says yes more than no,
Where the word "splendid" is a fine word,
With a hint of humor, to describe
Your revelations.
Where your revolutions
Were either won, half won,
Or found to be meaningless
Where the heart, now no longer reluctant to shine,
Does just that each dawn.
There you find yourself.

Jays

Those noisy birds before dawn—
"I'm trying to get back to sleep, ya know!"
Yet their beak-fight-sounds
For territory and mate
Keep me trance-like
Roaming though the dark house
From toilet, to table, to book,
Then back to bed again
With Lera's hip
Pressed against mine
While flickering on the ceiling I watch
Iraq dragged into war
Then back to the bright green grass
In the vacant lots around my studio
Near Whitman's house
In battered Camden, New Jersey,
Dawn like youth daily
Ending in old sunset.
We miss you Walt.
Your kindness toward all things
Of this world, even
Death.

The Moon at Dusk

The moon has a language
You can only understand
If you are in love with the moon.
The soft grey blue clouds
And yellow Claude Lorrain sunset
Translating the seen to the unseen.
But even the sky has its limitations,
The falconer's falcon knows
Its wildest circumference before
Heading back to arm and hood.

Once upon a time
Someone was given ninety years to live.
It almost seemed enough to untie
The million knots from birth
To love's benediction.
It almost seemed enough
To try to paint the blood of time,
On all fours, crawling to the door,
It almost seemed enough
To turn the whole body
Into a calm fare-thee-well.

August 20th

Each night I come out to swim
During the hot summer
To let mind and body float
In a shallow pool.
Crickets strike their legs together
In the ever-hum of seduction,
Nearby a neighbors air-conditioner rattles
Like a muffled factory night shift.
Flashing overhead jetliners
Glide one by one
Into Philadelphia Airport
Like slow, stale clusters of falling stars.
Underwater it all goes away
For as long as I can hold my breath,
Coming back only for air
And love.

10PM

The neighborhood lights go on
Behind blinds and drawn curtains,
A driveway light and a few porch
Lights beam in small globes. Some
Houses are completely dark
And their stillness is a hole in the air.
Between serene grape leaves bigger
Than my palm I can see through to our window
And the warm and cool yellow walls
Of our kitchen. During the day catbirds
Weave through these vines pinching
Grapes for ripeness. The slam
Of the old screen door has since been replaced
By a sliding one on rusty wheels.
This year the peaches have been best,
Sweeter and bigger. The pear tree
Is one-third brown leaves. I'm worried.
The garden looks silted
But could be just the August heat.
The idea, when we can,
Is to buy a farm to grow food
In earth and in a greenhouse all year.
It's getting harder and harder
To trust the sanity of the world.

Better to untie yourself on your own terms,
Say the wisest of the homeless.
Tonight you can smell autumn
A month away. Years seem to go by
More noticeably at the end of summer
As crickets herald in the changes
And afternoons begin to turn their backs to the sun.
Brown spiders turn up now sitting dead center
In intricate webs, some large as acorns.
I know one sunset each autumn
Will push melancholy right up against despair,
But then the past will be healed again for another year
With only its echoes heard down the corridors
Leading to the immediate and distant future.
As the new moon suggests,
Everything is always new.
You close your eyes for a moment, then
open,
To be reassured.

Way In

I don't know what to say
One just has to get out
Of the way sometimes.
Even so, your shadow
Will go with you like a long fuse
To a stick of dynamite
In an old Western;
Or a shadow, stretched out
On the grass, dreaming,
Or a quick shadow car thrown
On a dirty street across
A crushed can; or
An odd broken house
Of Popsickle sticks,
Or something
Terrifyingly accurate
About your foolishness

Way Out

Rain, wind, chill, tee shirt on, heater on
Driving mid-May way out
Down new unfamiliar streets in crumbling Camden
Inspired by the spirit of the old city soul
Stretching out on marble steps and lost voices
Like folded paper plane letters sailing out of windows.
The old rhythm of fine craftsmanship
Is the pace of walking down the street
With an eye for detail mixed with sunlight.
Some of the buildings are tired now
And lie down in the grass.

I WISH I COULD BE WISE
FOR MORE THAN A FEW MOMENTS
TO STAND STILL IN IT
BUT I KNOW IT WILL NOT BE
I WILL BE EXCITED PROMTLY
TO LIVE
BY SOMETHING SHINING AT ME
UNTIL ALL EXPERIENCE FALLS
FORGOTTEN IN SLUMBER
OR GIVEN UP
AND I SURRENDER TO BE A
MYSTERY AGAIN

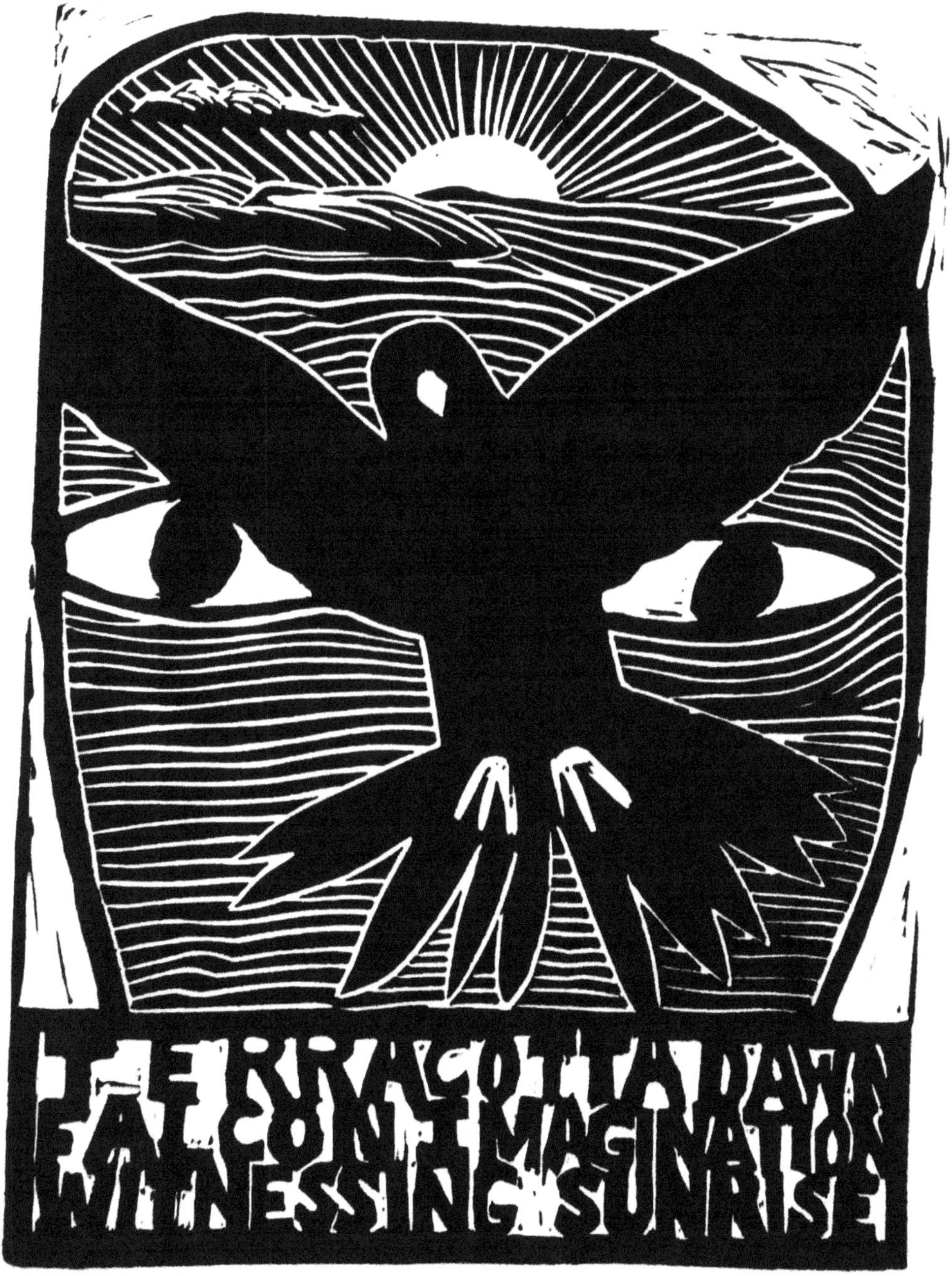
TERRACOTTA DAWN
FALCON IMAGINATION
WITNESSING SUNRISE

Farewell Dusk

The invisible wind

  Blowing my neighbors'

            Maple tree,

  Or is it dancing

On its own?

    Each
    Diaphanous leaf
    Glows radiant as gold sunset
      Streams though delicate membrane.

    How do we do it?
   Forgive
    Everyone
     Including
           Our—
        Selves.

It was just
    Confusion
In the strange land
      Of being born.

FAREWELL DUSK—

O the mind
on a slippery
    floor

Hidden Words

Another summer coming to an end,
We are eating the last of the tomatoes
With a little sadness, even as cooler nights
Inspire deeper sleep
and lovemaking.
Tomorrow my son goes back to school
And although I look forward to
Getting back to the anticipations of the studio
I will miss the wisdom of green grass, radishes,
Daylilies pointing to the sun,
And the voices of family.
Since my son was little
Every summer I've moved my studio home.
In the past bringing an etching press, potter's wheel,
To concentrate on those
Industries of the divine.
This year Black Eyed Susans
Flew in on the wind, seeding themselves,
Beginning a yellow patch. Over the summer
I painted two portraits and started seven sculptures,
But time mostly waned in matters of pragmatism.

The velocity of change
From waterfall to serene pool,
Like day to solemn dusk to evening.
Most of the year time is invisible,
But always one afternoon
In the beginning of September
There will be a melancholy
Burning in my eyes, the heart breaks
And does not tell the mind why.
So I sit at sunset, writing,
Drinking wine, until night
Hides the words.

Birthmark

I was born in the year of the horse
In the month of the horse
So it is easy for me to run
Across a great field,
But make no mistake
When I get to the other side
Or where I feel I'm suppose to be
My four legs can stand as still
As the corners of a temple.

A Possible Good-Bye

A black door is traveling through my mind
Like an eclipse covering the sun. I could
Lay down in that shape whispering good-bye
To all that I know.
The struggles line up so
Like train cars full of storms and desert.
When I was young I always won,
Whatever it was, even if I lost,
I won my loss.
I did not foresee how far it is
From then to now. Walking along
The top of a wall I slipped to one side.
I have to grow a new world
Out of my head.

Way In: Monday Morning, Week of Storms

After the heavy downpour
The wet tar road glazed black
Is covered by a low indigo sky
Wrapping cars in unnatural light.
Rain drops quiver just above
The wiper blade arc
At 30 mph. I know the pattern
Of flooded roads.
Around the circles at Brooklawn
The sticky mud of the tidal marsh
Is now deep under run off.
Discarded tires just break
The surface of the lake
Like the round backs of turtles.
Against the studio door
Light scratches to get in.
Unpacking lunch, the far away kindness
Of sunny earth; one avocado,
Dried fruit, nuts, chocolate, and cherry tomatoes
Bouncing like dud ping-pong balls.
An old record dusted off
Plays grumpy sounding
Ayurvedic chants
Cleansing the studio of bunk.

Does it work?
Indefatigable flower of mind
Buoyant in sensuality.

Backyard Clean Up

September garden refuse scattered in piles.
One last bowl of string beans
To fry up later with butter and walnuts.
I sit calmly with my back to the sun
At the edge of the world, art, academia.
People loiter under trees nearby,
The corner liquor store sells singles of Colt 45.
I can just see from my yard
One of the blue towers of the Ben Franklin Bridge
Merging with the blue sky,
And RCA's red brick tower, solitary
Above the small steps of skyline
Each night glowing with its stained glass dog,
And to the right, imposing,
The gray tombstone of City Hall.
At 9am down Third St.
A few cars roll or trucks rattle to the port,
The traffic light still changing
Above an empty roads austere serenity.
My studio was built in 1926
As a Union Hall, later was an Italian restaurant
During the Depression, was vacant in the 40's,
Then The Highway Baptist Church that moved on

By the time I bought it
Leaving behind its spirituals blending like a mixed cocktail
With the quieter echoes of patrons ordering Chianti.
Across the field I can make out Walt Whitman's house.
With a good arm you could throw a baseball
From my back yard to his.
I like being Whitman's neighbor, even if a century apart,
There is a dirt path between us in real and unreal time,
But a century has changed the city so much,
Changed in a way that even Walt would probably
Only recognize the people.

Acceptance

I accept it,
I am part
Of the disgrace,
My fingerprints
Turn up everywhere.

On TV
Refugees are on the move again,
Wheelbarrows filled
With their Grandmother's chairs
So by the road
Next to a broken wall
They can sit.

To redeem myself
I must be like an orchestra
That out of respect
Sits a very long time
Without playing.

* * *

I can't keep up with the reckoning
Tears from the past are still stinging in the air.
From ancient Egypt, old Greece, Africa,
Eastern Europe, even closer,
They brush against us in a summer's
Breeze when we are happy.
Can we push back?
What will we contribute?
Will our happiness be strong enough
To throw into the future
To sparkle interwoven with
The misery of history
That's so tangled like dirty rags
In each contemporaneous moment.

* * *

Climbing up and down the rocky slopes
Just to get to tomorrow
The poem like a blade,
with its benign use to open love letters.

Then for obvious reasons
Against those hunting you
Down for money.

    Or to wiggle a thin slice
    Through the skin of the world.
      To dig a little deeper
      To find the fact of light.

Way In: Saturday

Home

Under the pink cherry tree in bloom
Yellow daffodils with green sword leaves
Sway and bend as pavers
Wonder off between raised beds
Warming up to bat.
In caught
Fleeting moments
The flying color wheel
Of the garden;
Cardinal
Blue jay
Goldfinch.

Driving

Imaginative sky, the invisible
Just barely made visible
Making a funny face.

Studio

Paint cans scattered around
Like a beggar's drum kit.
Tick tock taps tops,
Even though the halo
Of the building
Is silence.

sOrrOw

Sorrow is everywhere
So what!
Try to find what is not sorrow.
Sparrows fly through the O's of
sOrrOw,
The incarcerated press between bars
On skinny canoes of the imagination.
Clocks tick joy and tock sorrow
And the day goes on riding
Its bicycle in the rain.
I am Houdini
Handcuffed to my sorrow
In a tank of water.

Posthumously Written Poem

How I loved sitting in the studio at dusk
All that Fall the days drawing in
Watching the sun fade to a coal
As the studio turned a beautiful grey
Calm as any Bodhisattva
Smiling at me as if to say — be still.
Gradually streetlights would lumber in
Their blunt rectangles of light
Shining across paint cans and junk stuff
To cast in silhouette animal faces
Across blank canvas.
Everyday a new darkness
Gathered under tables
Building black velvet cities.
I would sit for so long,
I could not move, the world
Was trying to tell me something
I could only hear at dusk
That now I know by heart.

Dear Despair,

I liked you better
When you were sorrow
Like a soft hand
Touching my knee
That has fallen since
Into clenched fingers.

It was always the distance
Between the little self
And the big self
Confusing us.

Everyone frightened
Of themselves or others
As if chaos was that close
To the heart.

We find our which-way slowly.
By our design the world is lonely.

Fra Angelico

I am beginning to love
Those yellow plates
Behind their heads.
In a painting by Fra Angelico
The haloes even follow
The severed heads
To a pile on the ground,
Sweetly painted in pastel colors
As if by an illuminated child.

By the time we get
To the energy and mysticism
Of Tintoretto
We are the drunken men
Of the new world.

Winter Morning

Cold mornings I ease away slow
To lubricate the engine, the heater
Kicks in ten blocks after dropping
Ben off to school, I drop him off
With a schoolboys cold red cheeks;
By the time I reach the studio
I'm like a log igniting in a woodstove.
Many things develop slowly like this,
I think I am one of them.
The road past the port, Bach
Blaring on the radio in a rattling truck
Seems to be laughing out loud with pleasure.
"Now" flips around into "won".
I've won something.
I'm flying through space on a springy seat
The winner of something
Taking the present with me
So there is never a future.

The Steps

The world falls across my steps,
Its gray images of brutality and **suffering**,
Thumps on worn steps down the block, too,
Rain or shine.

*

25 steps up to my studio
Multiplied by 15 thousand days,
Each step a wisp
Of primordial ascent and descent,
Until the cows come home.

*

The shadows of those slammed
Around the world or at home
Connect through back allies to our actions.
The pulled out accordion steps
we all slide down together
To a political cesspool.

*

The cellar steps squeak wicked **truth**
Until we find the light switch.

HEY   You might fail

A trillion dollars can buy a trillion dollar PEACE

A trillion dollars can buy a trillion dollar WAR

The next trillionaire that comes around the corner has a mighty big decision to make

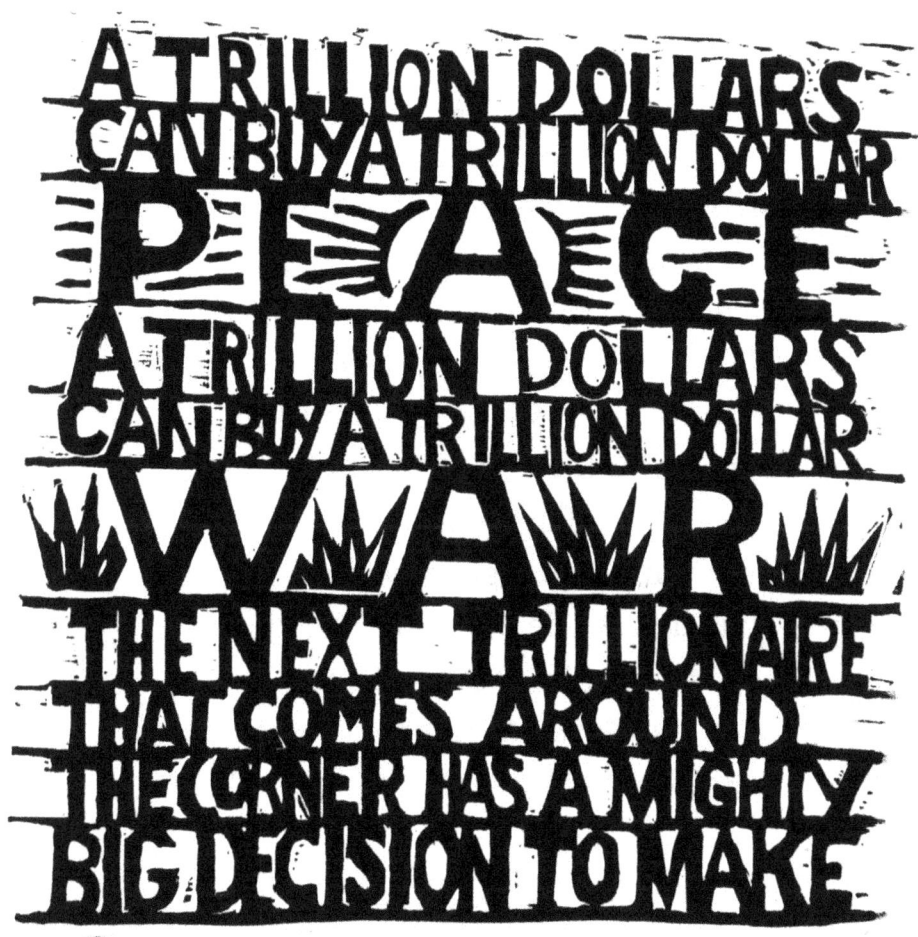

Cello Bits

I

I broke open the cello
To find the music
But only found the poetry
Of a broken cello.

II

Music has a big inside to it
But when I broke open the cello
It was small like a skull, infinite
When you close your eyes, but
Break it and it is a measured space.
Each morning Pablo Casuals played
The Bach cello concertos
And I imagine just to remind himself
That inside the cello and inside
The skull is the same space
Of no borders, giving reality
A kind of anti-gravity injection.

* * *

Listening to the opera always transforms the studio
Into a disheveled hotel suite along the Italian coast,
Circa 1930, its large windows
Facing the sea, the breeze
Secretly fox-trotting with the curtains
Behind the back
Of the old man there, his mustache
Like a clump of grass,
Listening to a scratchy La Boheme
After a days work in eternal light.
I am not sure how much I like opera
Or how much I just like being in that room
With the ghost-cloud of my grandfather
Signing with his hands.

The First Movement

The bows taunt gravity the violins are curved
In the fluid ways salmon wiggle upstream
That we follow gently into silence,
For a moment, after the first movement,
Then a cough and the shuffling of feet.

The empty glass we sneak in under our coat
We fill with the allegro so in the middle of the night,
Like The Middle Ages, if we wake, restless,
We have something to drink.

How are looking and hearing different?
Rembrandt, Copeland, or more important
How are they alike? Both are a password
Whispered to softened the world enough
From chain, to rope, to sewing thread,
Binding us.

The music is running down the street
We are chasing it all the way
From the Renaissance to now
Through music halls and radio waves.

The symphony, the song, not heard for so long,
It's as if we are another person listening
Almost to the point of having a new name.

I am, to be I was, I was to be I am.

Flea Market

The flea market has books that smell
But many more that don't.
On the table a world is lost to things
As if we were given a handful of jigsaw pieces
To invent the whole picture.

Junk and antiques exchange greetings
Like the rich and poor at a charity bazaar.

It's untenable, time pressed into
The weather beaten wood
While the thin line between the lips
Of the carved Saint espouses timelessness.

I slip from thought to thought.
Spring drowns everything in the current
From long before us to long after us.

I understand more when the sun is shining—
How to marry the earth.

Nowhere To Go

I

Nowhere to go
But to the two tone
Squeak back and forth
Of a child's swing
At the playground.

No place to go
But to let light
Struggle through
The quantum corridors
Of muscle.

Nowhere to go but to scrap on
Then stop and look
Like a crow transfixed
By glittering candy wrappers
Stuck in forsythia,
Then scrap on again.

Nowhere to go
But before the peach
Begging with each mouthful
To drip down your chin

To help spread it's
Igneous like seed.

Nowhere to go
But return like
The prodigal son
To the womb of forgiveness
And lift, now, into tomorrow
And another tomorrow,
Again and again until
There is no again anymore.

II

Nowhere to go
But to rattle along on the train
To buy brushes and paint.
Out of a tunnel, over a bridge,
Then back through a tunnel
Until up steps leading
To the hurrah of sky.

In the brightness I remember
How my sons were the sun
When they were young
With yellow hair,

Innocence lighting
The sacred candles
In their jumping legs
Glowing away darkness.

And my own vision, 13th street,
Momentarily, when I was
As young as a man could be
Before being called a boy,
The world a frieze of energy
An eternal breeze breezing
Through pedestrians
As readily as the walls of the buildings.
A mystery since
Has tangled up the world.

A city is made of stone, steel,
Wood, concrete, clay and flowers.
I did not grow up here
So I need green
To be the biggest color
I see out of any window.
Nowhere to go but into forever.

Beginning, Middle, End

I
beginning

        Coming out of the darkness
        Our headlights are still on
        To check the semi-dark road
        That is not so much a road
        But an invisible way
        Between our first nothing
        And our last nothing
        Where between we seek
        The juggernaut of hallelujah.

II
middle

        Centrifugal thoughts
        Spun out as if from a seed thrower
        Flying chips of life sputtering out to sow
        Consolation beyond dangerous sorrow.

III
end

        Hold on!
        I'm not there yet.

Maybe

I didn't know what to do,
I didn't know what bus to take,
What train ticket to buy,
What waterfall to go over a barrel in,
What dirt path to get lost on in memory,
What tree to climb to find its roots,
I didn't know what river to half drown in
As the ship sunk from chaos to slumber.

    The world is a trillion sparks.
    The world we see is carved out
    Of the world we don't see.
    They are guests of each other.

    I didn't know where to go
    As if I needed to go anywhere more
    Than a few hundred feet or through
    A handful of rooms to turn the world
    Inside out.

I am no longer an aggregate of Saint Despair.
I live in a new house in the body now.

The fired proof then lift the void that shapes water to drink

The past

holds

a knife

to your

head

to speak

the truth.

Hopscotch

Those who believe in hopscotch
Believe those blocks are the architectural
Foundation of innocence
Sturdy as any cinder block.
But how long do cinder blocks last?
Then each day
Sunset measures your shadow
When you walk to the park
With your dog
With a backpack of history.
Watch out everybody
The world will grab your hand
And put a knife in it
And you may drop it
Or say—
"I need this!"

So Be It

I turn around to see
The past staring back at me
Drilling holes through my deeds.

A jagged stone in a river
Tumbles over and over a haggard bed
Unhesitating in a torrent of current.

I loosen the hold of yesterday
By singing yellow back to the sun.

The dream of the rock
Is to become smooth.

The dream of the current
Is to be unimpeded.

The dream of men and women
Is to quit illusion.

The task of the world
Is to make a net

12.22.12

No one says what is
Has to be, but,
Because you can not
Save the world,
Save yourself.
How?
Somehow.

1. Move to Camden, NJ.
   Buy a big old building
   Renovate on miserly budget
   Weather the hardships
   And make art for the rest
   Of your life because that
   Is the most exciting thing
   You can do.

2. Up to you
   P.S. Don't forget
   The world

1987 My Broken Down Building / Paid in Full

"**Dancing up and down**

The steps to the studio

Like Fred Astaire"

Mar. 12

It's harder to leave the studio now
Even to go canoeing in the Pine Barrens.
Those days, half way down the river
We'd stop for picnics, the bunch of us.
A young music student, Meredith, sang opera
By the cedar water surrounded by green.
We read poetry and ate olives
With French bread. On hot days we swam
In the orange tinted stream.

I never knew how to paint its tight branches
Preferring the shore, the sky
That waded way out to sea
Reflecting the occasional turbulent clouds
I felt deeply.

The pines create silent rooms,
That is part of what the studio is now,
That is why I think of them.
A sandy path through light and dry air
Nourishing trees that have grown
And changed slowly over the years,
The way I have been slowly changing.

Summer Nights

After midnight insects talk
Their click language.
Humidity gets me out listening
To the continuous low roar
Of distance highway traffic
And the soft ripple sounds of water
Stirred in a chlorinated pool.
A new moon drifting in and out
Of cloud animals
Casts its occasional spotlight
On the ladder to exit naked,
A middle-aged man with
The complexities of life to go back to bed.
I can see the dark sky about to fall
Into my hands that would foreshadow
A shadow across canvas,
But a handful of glittering fireflies intervene
And it seems instead that I am walking through stars.
Submerged in water, I believe in everything,
Finding one thing true then only
To find a lurking truth in it's opposite.

It makes for a kind of casual reality
Where five storey high suburban oak trees
Are not so much our ancestors but cousins.
We are all new here on what was a cornfield
That was farmed for a hundred years,
Then before that, woods far back,
And before that, mystery.

Student Days Still Life Hours

Eventually tabletops became landscapes
Loaves of bread were cathedrals
Casting transparent shadows
Down alleyways between
Old farmhouse bowl
And cucumber.

I grew up on these streets
Meditating on plums
With moonlight floating
Across the surface
And storms lurking behind
The broken Chinese lute
By the dead fish.

The terrain of youthful melancholy.
Sunrise a lemon.
Sunset a pomegranate.

Painter

I am a figure painter
Not because I understand the body,
But because I do not understand the body.
There is more of you I don't see than see, the stars
Glittering in a dark underneath of soft flesh. How
Lovely strange to touch you for real, the universe giveth,
13 billion years to make resolute your distinction, and
Yet still you are like the splashed beads reflecting
other beads in a waterfall.
Time is sentimental. Matter is crazy.
I just want to sit and look for a while
At your
Hand the
Color of
A loaf
Of bread.

Tintoretto

I

I sit on the edge of my seat
Wondering if I am going sane
Or insane
As the rain blows
In scribbled lines
Across the trees.
The world rushes by
Into nothingness where
Only light shines
Sweeping away what most
People find meaningful.
Young in Venice
I was a sparrow flying
In the twilight skies
Of the vaulted ceilings
In the San Rocco.
Now I am a crow
In a rambling studio
In Camden, New Jersey,
Still scavenging
Form and color
To take back to the nest.

II

Just out of school,
Sunlight illuminating the Piazza
As the shadow of the Campanile
Untied geometry from superstition.
Under shaded arches, cool
As Shangrila, Italians
Sang their words ordering Chianti.
Radiating out from the center,
Narrow passages still held
The footsteps of candle lit Italy.
Red geraniums above
Tumbled out the cages
Of wrought iron balconies.

Raw Tintoretto, almost
Vulgar with impatience
To finish as the next painting
Flooded his brain.
Highlights on drapery like quick
Lightening bolts in a storm.
Sublime Titian threw him
Out of his studio.
Energy is eternal delight

Echoed Blake in everyone's
Head who read it.
Generations later all this would descend
Onto paintings on velvet.

The rippling water.
As light is both particle and wave
It is both science and spirituality
Reflecting the lagoon and Bridge of Sighs.
The shaking world
Of reflections.
All is divine or nothing is divine.
Either way, all is equal.

A mother and child is singular.
The Madonna and Child
Is the compressed overlapping
Portrait of every mother and child
In human history, as the Crucifixion
Is suffering no more or less
Than every soul burned in Iraq
Incited by an inept government
Corrupt as the worst of the Medici.

More often
The world changes slowly
As a body does.
Customs, music, come and go,
Rise and fall as flesh
Is buried then reborn
Into sturdy trees.

The best fireworks of Venice
Threw glitter all the way
Into Renoir's late paintings.
A frame pulled away
From a Tintoretto revealed
An inch border of raucous purple
Hidden from soot and sun for ages,
Now scrambling to the 21st century.

In the extravaganza
Of veined marble floors and columns,
The nascent birth
Of the paintings, along
With velvet drapery and over
The top hosiery, and
In ermine robes all the cries
Of animals mistreated.

And only the finest
Beautiful white linen
As Tarquin rushed toward
Lucretia with gleaming knife.

We are no longer who we were,
Of course not—
That would be a stagnant river.
We must unwind forward
Into the beings of who
We are not now.

In the Basilica of Byzantine mosaics
Cups and plates slide off upturned tables.
Even an honest heart
Could not nail them down.
Perspective was the arrow
Shot straight through the cerebral cortex
To the vanishing point
Miles into a canvas.
Doors opening out
To the picture plane
Became swinging doors
That led inward.

III

One night, homesick, drinking
Cheap wine in a pension
Sharing glass after glass
With the owner in conversation
Of smiles and gestures
And like sounding words understood
And misunderstood,
I tell him I am a papa.
My son was two at the time.
His quizzical look, then
An argument in pantomime,
I am a papa, Papa.
Only later did I realize
In translation, I was telling him
With all the drunken conviction
Of youth, that I was the Pope.

The Massacre of the Innocence
Of 1583, fourteen
By nineteen feet.
The spectral shafts of light
Intuit the Futurists
Who wanted to burn it down.

I miss the relevancy of painting
Outside the current horse race
Of economic value.

Ascetic Tintoretto,
Humble in everything except his art.
Furthest from the center of Venice
On the point of a triangle with Titian
And Veronese rooted near the aristocracy.
His cloaked figures have their way
Of swaying forward and backward
In faithful supplication
As ceremoniously joy of mind
Greets sorrow of mind.

IV

I wondered around remote Venice
Searching for the quietest places
Where light could transcend stone,
No one seemed to notice, just another student,
Profoundly still in a beautiful city
Like someone looking at the future
A million years from now.

Way In

Second floor, morning, and first thing
Is the blank silence of snow falling
And sunlight wading through the studio's
Windows and doors.
Sculptures of my Egyptian-like
Kings and queens saturated with color
Ride in their permanent state of meditation.
Cinderblock walls filter
The far away sounds getting closer
Of birds I cannot see.

A million years have happened on this spot
And more, almost to the point where you could say
An eternity has happened on this spot.

The first hawk I ever saw in the city
Was sitting on a telephone wire
Across from my balcony
The size of a cocker spaniel.
I watched as still and quiet
As any terrified prey
Until it flapped clear into the air,
But more frequently the slow moving gulls
Afloat high in the air coming in from the Delaware

And maybe going straight through to the Atlantic
Over the Pine Barrens
Of wild Christmas trees.

An Intricate Pattern

The yellow roses are in tattered bloom
This late summer. I sit in the shadow
On my studio
By the marble step table
From 3rd and Washington,
The building long gone,
That I paid four drunken men
To push here in a cart.
A healthy breeze shakes the loose parts of the world,
All the leaves
Point to the wind getting away
Like a thief stealing a calm day.
I am stranded in drowsy
Afternoon thought letting
Silkscreen ink dry before
Another color is applied.
That tangled web
Is like a picture of my last
Ten thousand heart beats.

Rain

Gentle rain
Dry soil says
Here is the key to my house

What if...

What if the train was made of speed?
(Speed made the train to express speed)
What if your family were there
The moment you needed them most,
What if all the objects on the table broke
In an earthquake and you watched
All their light escape, what if
A stranger felt more like a brother,
What if the wind was music after all,
What if desire turned itself into love,
What if kissing a neck was
The playful salvation, what if
You saw someone a block away
That was the future person you would be,
What if you stood too near the edge
Of a cliff then turned your back on death,
What if each pump into a willing other
Was the rung of a ladder climbed
To the height of loving union,

What if we could see the stars each night
The way they shone throughout antiquity,
How would that remake you,
What if the world blew up
But was still there as before,
More significant or insignificant.
What if the world implied yes more often
Than the hoods of oppression,
What if reality lost its credibility
And the inside of the apple
Was your new home?

Pool

My eyes slowly adjust to the midnight world
As moonlit honeysuckle flowers wrap the redbud trunk
And underbrush cluster of vines entwine
Like a shuffled Tarot deck predicting complications.
The water's warm floating, my eyes and nose just above drowning
To witness a handful of stars connected to us by strings of light.
In black silhouetted leaves are tall tales where all the words
Are rearranged but have a hint of reason,
And from time to time, a thumb and mitt or the male and
Female of a jigsaw puzzle will snap together and a small portion
Of sense will appear reflecting its greater surroundings
The way the carapace of a drop of water does.
Night heads for morning down a gravel road, its taillights
Like the red fading coals of sunset that will turn around
Soon to become the glowing headlights of dawn.
Inward and outward the seeming conflict
A thin layer of skin the barrier
Between two infinities.

As a Kid

As a kid,
Whether in the back yard
Or in rows along the bike path,
Trees were always my numberless
Benefactors.

No matter how lost I was
The invisible bridge back
That I could just barely see
Was made of wood.

And in the heyday of age ten,
Scampering like a monkey
To the top of the willow tree
That held me to see Philadelphia
Some twenty miles away.

But what I was really doing
Was looking at the chain link fence
Of the sky
That held the body back
While the imagination slipped through.

The Canoe of Our Bones

I

As if the river had
Compartments of time
Day by day went by.
So, there is both
In the one thing shining,
The sense of the long
Thread of the river
From mountain to sea
As it passes in
The footsteps of hours.

II

Our three-year-old hand
Is still in our hand, even
Now, whatever age,
The way the third ring
In a tree is still there
As it grows outward
Thriving like the
Momentum of fireworks
From spring to autumn's
Incandescent leaves.

III

The river's edge
Can stray
Swishing around
In eddies,
In whirlpools
That curl around
The events of the day
Hugging them
With attention.

IV

There is no other day
Then today. Always.
The past is naught
The future sought,
Oh hell, we know all this
In the canoe of our bones.

Auto-Portrait

When I was young I was untied like a boat
And allowed to drift without instruction
On living and dying. I made it back and forth
Across the sea a few times and through
Tangled thoughts strode a kicking horse.
I drifted through fragments of heavens
And hells around me like they were broken
Stained glass windows. Down the same
Street from the hospital where I was born
I made it to the studio where I was reborn
Without hesitation to a quiet life
Of the desired work.
I watch light.
Each year birds return with small
Globes of renewal. I am conservative
Up to a point where I am a heretic.

An Old Photograph

We were there. The past was there, too,
Both walking forward, we didn't see then
How far it would go, to be today.
The pleasure of so many moments that left
And still they leave behind a trail of lighted candles,
That's how you can find me in the dark.
And all along the way, the earnestness of study,
Disciple made wings,
Though the world was still heavy.
In the black and white photo with period scalloped edges,
Proof, if I ever needed it, that I was there, or here,
To use like an out-of-date passport to cross borders
Into the future, to places that don't exist
Until you get there.
The captured clouds in the photograph
Foretold change. The clouds were philosophers.
The kids grew up to be old men and women.

Snow Day

A muffled car horn
Heard through unique crystals
Of whirling snow.
In a faded orange shirt
Pacing like a goldfish
Behind the picture window
I wonder if I will make it through seven miles of snow
To under the roof, leaking in two spots,
Of my rag-a-muffin studio.
Relax and see,
Have another cup of coffee,
Let the mind write love letters,
Be a philosopher,
Write this poem.

Inside a snowflake is the future of architecture.

Beauty is Saint Equilibrium's wisdom.

Even Rimbaud's, "One evening I sat
Beauty on my knees and found her bitter,"
Is beautiful.

Maybe beauty is to remind us
We never give up, but like sunlight
That even at night just shines someplace else.
Maybe, but now I only hear
The long way off silence
Of the studio like a block
Of hushed anticipation
Waiting for my day to day life
To stomp in the door
With wrath and apparitions.

Wet Feet

1

The world seems to fall away as if someone important
Said it was just illusion, though not faster than you want
It to fall. This synchronicity is something like the pact
that you can not out race your reflection in a mirror.
The mind whips up confusion
Just as well as the world can, becoming more dearly beloved
As the light in things gets turned on or wind is seen blowing
Even in still objects, trying to reveal themselves
Like the earthly way you step out of your robe, then
In the unearthly way known to lovers, out of your skin.

2

Across my chest your palm weighs six ounces. Your fingers
In a kid's game pretend to be legs strolling up and down my arm
Like someone musing along the shore, half happy, half sad,
But content at the wiggled edge between land and sea with wet foot
Prints smothered out by each wave bubbly
                      at the furthest stretch onto land

Before drawing back, somersaulting shells,
                              chased by sandpipers
Again and again. That appearing repetition
And low hum of niggling revelation
Becoming so resolutely configured in your mind
Of the world saying hello and goodbye to itself.

Nettled Flower

The Concrete Body Made of Light

Even though I can see, I half live my life by touch,
Or hearing, the wind rustling me into night,
Ruffling clothes sliding to the floor
Then the whole hot length of your body
Against mine. In all directions the universe
Is expanding for millions and millions of light years,
But here even our knees kiss by their nearness.
Our hips press together the doorknobs
Of our upper femurs as if they could open
By a simple clockwise twist
To the whole interior of the body.
If I could not see, being
Held by some circumstance of darkness,
I would flail my arms around to find you.
My arms would slice through you if you were
Light alone, so I heed, lovingly,
To the condensation of energy to matter
Like frost on a windowpane
Looking out into eternity.
In celebration of touch I light candles
Like an ancient miner climbing out
Of his tunnels, or loops of turmoil,
Back to daybreak, back to
Dawn light describing curved

And jagged shape that magically,
Or majestically, is modeled form.
The concrete body made of light,
Even those clods of dirt
As kids we called dirt-bombs
Because if heaved as high
As ten year old muscles
Could heave they would always
Hurtle back to a hardness
Like pavement as we watched
Them burst into dirt smoke.
Even those good for nothing
Clumps of dry earth are light
Filled bulbs exploding
Light into light. And Oh,
"O", that antiquated poetical
Exclamation of awe, wonder.
With your permission if I could use it
This once. "this heaven floating
Around us, O this radiant
Heaven we become
When we slip from our
Life-life to our death-life".

Flying Carpet

High Point Trail, February Residency, Peter's Valley

Blue distance
Through winter trees
Across the valley,
Scraggly pines
Hold small snowballs
In their needles.
Brittle leaves in chattering clumps
The wind ignited to conversation.
The marked trail for well-wishers like me.
Looking west the blue serpentine
Delaware River curves its snake body
Between New York and Pennsylvania.
Standing still the last crunch of snow sound
Goes home with the wind.
Overhead the crow's solitude
And mine without complaint.
There are no answers
To no questions.

Like a Full Moon

A destroyed deer, twisted by roadside.
An old woman lay one more time in her bed
Before being moved to eternity. Each past
Year is hurried into a carved wood cyst inside us
In the countdown to New Year's Eve.
Death tries to starve the living with sorrow,
Its pitiless centuries, its brutal today, the ones
We would miss down to our bones
If it would happen too soon, until, after years of
Labyrinth making and unmaking
Wise sorrow turns up empathetic
And the whole world then seems an act of prayer.
The trees in prayer, the stones in prayer,
The silhouettes of many man and woman
With head bowed,
The frog in prayer with snake,
The lake with prayer with muddied
Catfish. Afternoon light the prayer with long
Shadows for the unknowable to reach out
Of the unknown to shake peace around us;
Its almost brazen luminosity,
Shining toward the unsettled self
In its near catastrophic darkness.

Fever Day 3

The water sounds like static
In the electric kettle right
Before boiling. The heater
Kicks in in the basement
Its muffled sound comes along
With the heat. I was sick
Yesterday and yesterday's yesterday.
Today I'm not sure.
It's cold and overcast outside
And the damp is entering
My head. Is that it?
I never considered myself
One of those who becomes
The weather, but I suppose
I'm sunnier on a sunnier day.
Making tea has tired me out.
That means I'm only on the mend,
Not mended, lightheaded.
That couch with folded up blanket
Looks good, like a woman
About to wrap me in her arms.
She is dizzy with silly.

"Hey, come here, come here,"
She's winking at me,
"I need a sad violin,
A sad violin."

The Request

To be still, as if it were always so,
Somewhere in mind and body,
Way back, away from clamoring approaches,
The whirling counter clockwise world
Manifestly obliged to corruption.

The unblocked soul can say, "here I am"
Untouched by the knives,
A tooth sticks into the rim of Nirvana
Eating a spring onion.

Oh simple straightforward world
Stay at my side a little longer
Before you turn
Again to mayhem.

The News

The world said something sad to everyone,
Some didn't hear it and kept on being happy.
The world repeated its sadness and everyone heard
This time. Some had a reservoir of joy with the world
And so did not break even when they cried.

Some in the crowd only knew sorrow
And some only joy, and some knew,
Almost reverently, how one
Half-way always overlaps the other.

There was a smile. The world walked
Over to a child whispering the way the sun
Walks over to whisper to a seed.
A long time ago that was you, remember,
A child talking to the sun.

Scaffolding

The scaffold like an inner shadow of bones holding us up
That we've made from experience to protect us, if it could,
Against a future we expect, is sometimes made of steel,
Or wood, but maybe the workman of the mind who can see
Behind the door we can only sleep-dream to get to got it wrong,
As we twist ourselves forward, and it should have been made
Of water so it could take the shape of each moment. It's a dare,
Almost a physical dare, with consequences like in reckless
Adolescence jumping between rooftops, for anyone to break
The pattern of bridges built from the past to now,
Which ones should or shouldn't hold tight,
Which ones originated in darkness
And could withstand the freight of a chugging locomotive.
I watch sentences reach out, expectantly, strain
                                                as if a rock weighed
The center of them, their ends tied to opposing riverbanks.
There is always a complexity in and around the body,
No one wants a bridge they can't understand
Or a sentence that doesn't take you ashore.

A History of Landscape

The first kiss with the sky
Still lingers on. I see it
Each day in my life
And in Constable's paintings.
It is turmoil first
Unraveling itself into
A peaceful expanse.
Do we look at the sky
Or through it
Into our own
Spontaneous sky athwart
With disparate
Passions.

And I am still
On the edge of my seat
Looking at the carved
Clouds like rocks
In El Greco
With their emerging blue skies
Of crushed lapis-lazuli
Representing
The sincerest
Infinity.

Museum

The other paintings and sculptures in the room
Slump to polished academia near Chardin's
"Basket of Plums".

I've painted many still lives early on
Where I wanted a profound stillness
In the movement of time.
For some of them, I think,
The endeavor had merit.

Lunch Time Poem

His heart was in the open
Before Hiroshige's wave approaching the shore.
A thunderstorm in the background
Grew smaller and smaller until it just floated
Above the horizon like a purple flower.
His heart then stood up on the sand
Without a bathing suit.

Under

      under
  the scatteredness
        and exasperations
            that toss
    the world
I can be quiet
forgetting the mind is
    a mind
    for awhile
before being hurled back
    to memory
        and sensation.

I can sit calmly
  in candle lit
      wavering illumination
flicking back
      the serrated edge
  of
    encircling night
as if inward trepidation
    and outward trepidation
were reaching forever
      toward each other

    buffered only by
        this hallowed flame.

I can sit sturdy
       as tree roots
with scepter; illuminate graphite,
   dashing notations
          of brutality
   kindness
in the limelight of paper.

Mandala

The beautiful sand paintings
That get brushed away —

Over time
Even your favorite
Rembrandt
Is a mandala.

Opening the Window

Opening the window a wondering
Sorrow or the wind
Unsettles everything settled in.
Or so unmoved in a quite while,
A dust covered book,
And old ways of thinking
Coded in our fingerprints
That all along have been
Leaving behind a thin oily film
Of who we are on everything
We've touched.

Ruffled papers on the floor,
The wind or sorrow said so,
Leave them there until
A significant collection
Of scuffled footprints
Mark them real.

Perspective

The straight road proceeds to its logical
Conclusion of a vanishing point.
I draw a winding stair and think of Yeats.
Fence posts in succession leading away
Each seem to be pounded a little deeper
Into the earth. A circle lies down
In the oblong circumference of
An earthenware plate.
You can plot shadows too, but maybe
Better letting them be the suggestive
Darkness they always are.
A razor casts a sliver of that darkness,
Like the slot at the back
Of a 1950's medicine cabinet
Where my father pushed
His used razor blades into oblivion.

Starting Out and Continuing

1

In the beginning of my work,
Painting, when sometimes
It seemed the abracadabra
Of a picture
Or the humility of a picture,
I wanted a painting so quiet
People would walk by it first
Then slowly come back as if
They forgot their keys, or gloves,
Or something, only to be quiet, too,
They and the painting being quiet
Together for a while.
I remember one with a pear
And bowl on a green Persian
Style rug laid over a table
Painted after my grandfather
Died. It was the quietest painting
I think I ever did and I'm sorry
I sold it but I was young and
Needed the money. I watched
Them carry his body down
The steps under a cloth as the
Red and blue fireworks of the
Ambulance blinked across our faces.

It was a Memorial to this English
Gentleman though I didn't plan it
That way. I never know what
A painting means until after
It's done, and sometimes long after.
My grieving came out in deep greens
And ivory black.
With so many years along now,
I feel like I have flown around
The world a few times with
New possibilities of one's work
And self, which of course, are
Interchangeable.

I feel another
Series of still lifes coming on
The way some people think
They are coming down with the flu.
I have always lived my life
Out of chronological order
Or at least it has felt so.
The beginning can come back
Again, and again and again,
And the beginning can be the
End and the end can be the middle.

To the next paintings—
Let me speak to you honestly,
Surprise me with a step toward
Where I've never been.

2

In night is the birth of day,
In day is the birth of night,
In joy is the birth of sorrow
In sorrow is the birth of joy.
Everything turns this way
By slow or fast rotations,
Unevenly paced. To be held
In sorrow for an hour, a day,
Or weeks before joy shines.
Or elated by joy only to
Be admonished by the lost
And broken on Broadway
As you are being followed
Melodically block by block
In a busted-up city by Samuel
Barber's Adagio for Strings.

Labyrinth

"Rattle, rattle", the wind talking to loose panes in the door.
Outside juvenile crows with keen blue eyes are ravenous,
Curious, watching thrown away black plastic bags from single malts
Swoon in updrafts that look hesitantly for a moment, like small
Holes in the sky. Inside the studio's full of conflict
And the solution of conflict. It is full of broken pieces of the world
Like a hospital of things.
I race silence through the maze,
The impatience of my patience
Is to be both rat and labyrinth.
From the corner of my eye I watch the city burning down
One building at a time to be replaced by a new city
One building at a time.
It is pain going forward and adventure,
For things, for people.
We are flames within ourselves, too,
Burning into a new city.

Hat

On the hat I wear
On the inside of my head
I've pinned a crow's feather.

When I stand on the edge
Crow spirit feels at home
As if I were to jump off and fly.

But I could just as well
Tumble down a steep cliff.
I still don't know yet.

My life seems to go in slow motion.
Today I'm leaning way over the rail
Looking both up and down
At the immense distance each way.

A Day

A man walking into the garden
Becomes the garden, his thoughts
Temporarily like gentle columbine
Bending with the deliberate gestures
Of a fluorescent butterfly.
Under-all, holly, peach, pear,
Apple, fig, able roots stretch
In the dung fueled earth
Worming to their outermost
Fate bound in solemnity.

A broken mind is patched up
With yellow rays, a brown acorn
Splits the ground
To rapture in the sun
For a hundred years.

The mockingbird, fidgets,
Weighs each plump, fleshy
Grape plucking the heaviest
To excrete the seeds
In splotches.

Night is at the end of the street,
But if you walk slowly
Attentive to loves lowliest
Enactments
The day appears to stretch
So far forward and so far back
That even time seems to say
"Farewell time."

Amazement

Overcast sky, other
Nights light pollution.
I have to drive five
Hours to see the sky
Like any privileged
Man, woman or child
Could in 1920. What
I want is to be aware
On my nothingness
And perfection reflected
In the God-sky of stars.
Each night my sandal soles
Or feet souls
Kiss the ground
In steps

As the stars cajole—
You are nothing
And everything, how
Can that be?
The stars, I can
Read their mind.
"If my glow sprinkling
Bounty was evermore
Present in your life,
Out kitchen windows,
Head back yawning
Late night walk, you
Would move
More through amazement".

The Clock

The clocks are not always accurate about time.
Behind the clock face is our face we don't recognize
Looking down at us before we were born.

And the face far ahead, we can only recognize
By the compassion we had for our mother, our
Grandmother, moving in times oblivion,
We can now see waiting for us to arrive.

To Salem

The clouds are to beautiful today
To care about ambition.
The uninterrupted sun a magical warmth
On the left side of my face
Driving south through trunk and branch
Shadows over the road then a huge
Square patch under a bridge
Like a pool filled with night.
A glint on the road ahead,
Maybe a quarter, I call heads,
Seems to say yes to any situation
Just around the corner
I'm driving seventy mph toward.

A.G.

Everyone knows Amazing Grace
That's why someone wrote it
That's why bagpipes play it
That's why a President
Sang it to America
That terrible day of weeping
And suffering
And because a crowd
Makes money on that issue
Nothing will change

Resistance

I close my eyes to resist the world
To let sound build awareness around me.
Quiet cars come closer, louder, then fade away.
Every leaf rustles hello, then in a moment, goodbye.
Bird song meant to defend territory
Is comforting to those without skin in the game.
Muffled voices pass close
Whispering under distant yelling kids at tag.
No sunset rays reach the bench
Of my leaf thick retreat.
No dogs barking. When the wind stops,
When no cars, and everyone safely home
For dinner, now comes the immense
Empty of sound sky like seamless night,
A harbinger of what you bring to it, indifference or love.
But I want to open my eyes again as if they were legs
Running through the world. This returning, again
And again, after so many different departures, close and far,
Tangible and intangible, so many footsteps in untrodden sand.
The alchemy of turning gold into the world.

Youth

In body or mind
REVOLT AGAINST
The old world that never
Worked for **HUMANITY**
That never worked
For the **EARTH**
That will never work
For your **FUTURE**

July 5

The sun straining through pine needles
Takes the edge off 95 degrees.
Watershed creek up to your knees deeper
At the bend under the rope swing.
Kids rattle around like toy guns with pop sounds,
Dogs shout at each other every chance they get.
A few families come to this broad curved beach
In the Pine Barrens the tail end of a three day
July 4th weekend. As you swim the iron rich creek
Turns everyone gold with its faux Midas touch.
The night before fireworks banged and clamored
Above the Delaware, sparkled in reflection across wave tips.
Smelled smoke drifted as a grey blanket and as you watched
It seemed to contract into bits as if a history of tattered,
                                                        beaten flags,
A country born out of violence and tumult.

America the Beautiful?

I hear on the radio
Two stocks get a strong buy,
Tiffany's and The Dollar Store.
If you ask America for directions
It will point this way —
A hundred thousand people
To buy something for a dollar
And one person to buy something
For a hundred thousand dollars.

T V

I watch the news
Some people with great success
Others without.
I am closer to those without,
Our kinship of personal
Hardship. But away from
The world my success
Is the star I follow
With search light eyes.
My very heartbeat
With its warm jets
Of imagination,
Un-subsiding
In the clamps of the world that say
You should be this
You should be that
You should breathe money.

Gloucester City Memorial

The only way to have stopped
The Second World War
Was not to have
The First World War.
Who is courageous enough
To not have a war?
Names on a small town
Monument, the shocks
And trembling long ago
Takes your heart
Out to sea
On the calm water
That eternity loves
Then back again to the dates
And names inscribed on
A bronze verdigris wall
Where by the base grows
A real flower in real time
You can touch because
You are alive and older
Then they ever were.
The young ones
Up against the Kaiser.

We walk with one eye
On sorrow and one on grace
Until our own name finds
Its resting place.

Black Horse Pike and Kings Highway

I am first in line at the red light.
Far ahead I see a box coming
Twinkling red, white and blue lights
As if it were the start of a July 4th parade,
But it's winter.
With the green light we all know
The road is off limits to move until
The flashing box decides its way,
Ambulance written across the back.
I feel brother to all who waited
For the one in more need
To glide more easier to whatever
Their fate might be,
For a moment we were a community
Of compassion and fear for our own
Vulnerability.

From Silence

Sometimes, wonderfully exhausted, a day already

Preparing for tomorrow, the studio dark as a subway tunnel,

In my head a moth of queries comes drawn to the halo

Around the streetlight and what cannot be understood

By the mind gets acknowledged by stalwart nerve.

> Reclining on her side
> Her arm was the length
> And color of a briquette
> In a pose resting across
> Her scrutinized torso,
> Pinching a breast.

The reality of the painting we get is usually

Insufficient to the reality of the painting we seek.

    The casual outline of her bare shoulder we know

    Does not really exist but is part of the bed,

    The wall, the moon. The world is not just the world

    Anymore, it has roots beyond all reason.

Sequence

Night

All the crickets chirping late August
Surging with clicking legs their song
"Find me my love"
Their meaning of life is not our meaning
Until the descent to the base
Of our stacked chunks of spinal bone
Or deep inside the mush of exoskeleton
To where our common flag waves,
Our common denominator
Of procreation, to live
And be outlived.

Morning

The holy dawn, or such like, midweek,
Or any day if your head's in the zone
Mine not always is.
Outside the early shrill of cicadas
Their chorus passing through us in waves
"It is our duty to live"
Or more precisely like ocean swells passing
Through us, lifting us off the sandy bottom
Before setting us back down

As we waded out past
The breaking waves.
Then blunt
Further rackets of the morning,
Mower, weed-wacker,
Sometimes a chainsaw chewing through
A teetering branch across a driveway
Spewing sawdust down to show
Our temporary state of order
Juggled with the general mess of things.
Looking at our reflection in a mirror
We don't see ourselves
But we see a tangled world
That all of us made.
Afternoon comes flipping
A coin and you call heads.
It's all still spinning midair.

The Sea Is Writing Its Autobiography

Faded driftwood color
Like a fresco the sea painted
I would love to throw
My son's old alphabet blocks
Into the spiraling waves
If I could be sure to
Reclaim them
Five years down the pike
Washed up and washed
Out on shore. What would
They spell on their own
With their corners the rocking
Lullaby sea rounded smooth.
By fortuity the sea
Is writing its autobiography
Up and down the coast
With washed up broken chairs,
Chipped shells and grievous
Bedlam, but since
It's our autobiography, too,
So our bones say, and our bones
Know where we came from, we sit
On the beach reading thrillers, glossy magazines and
Any other beach comfort fluff

While surreptitiously
Being whispered to
By time before time.

Morning

Moments take
Just a moment to pass
With neither the feeling
Of being too slow
Or too fast.
I like these mornings
The porch wearing light
The birds fastidious.
In newspapers I wade through
The deceit and treachery of government,
More so during a war.
But the garden
Says something different
About the gift of the world.

Hi Dog

Around the corner from home
On a suburban road
My dog's head hanging
Out the car's back window
A little girl skating, sees,
Waves, says hi…hi…
My eyes widen
As if
All the innocence of the world
Was suddenly
Turned on
By a switch
Shining on everything
For the next quarter mile

www.ingramcontent.com/pod-product-compliance
Lightning Source LLC
Chambersburg PA
CBHW080451170426
43196CB00016B/2755